Start Your Investment Journey
A Personal Finance Playbook

Table of Contents

Chapter 1. Introduction

Introducing "Start Your Investment Journey: A Personal Finance Playbook"-- a special report designed to make the complex world of investments seem as simple and exciting as a trip to your favorite amusement park! Beginner? No worries! Seasoned investor? It still packs a punch! This report is your financial adventure at your fingertips. With the ease of a conversation over coffee, it navigates the often intimidating terrains of the investment world, right from the basic building blocks to advanced strategies, all designed with the objective of making you the master of your financial future. Get ready to turn the page, and embark on an exhilarating investment journey. It's not just a report, it's a roadmap to your wealth creation. So don't wait, this is the cheerleading push you need to secure a financially independent future!

Chapter 2. Understanding Personal Finance: Basics to Begin

Personal finance services as the cornerstone of one's financial journey. Let's peel back the layers of this complex but necessary field and delve into its basics. It all begins with understanding some fundamental concepts - income, expenses, savings, and investments - and then we navigate through the essential aspects of budgeting, emergency funds, insurance, taxes, and retirement planning.

2.1. Income: The Starting Point

Income is the money you earn. It can be in the form of a salary from your job, rental income from property, returns from investments, or income from a business. Take note, not all forms of income are steady or guaranteed. For instance, bonuses and profits from investments can fluctuate.

Knowing your total income gives you an idea of how much money you have at your disposal. Look into all your avenues of income and sum it up to get a clear idea of your financial bandwidth.

2.2. Expenses: The Necessary Drain

All the money you spend constitutes your expenses. These can be divided under:

1. Necessities - Rent/mortgage, groceries, utilities, healthcare, transport

2. Discretionary expenses - Dining out, vacations, entertainment

3. Financial goals - Savings or investments, retirement funds

Categorizing your expenses helps identify where your money is going which is vital while preparing a budget.

2.3. Savings: The Safe Harbor

Savings refer to the portion of your income not spent on expenses. It provides a buffer for emergencies, big-ticket expenses, or as a pool for future investments. Experts often suggest a rule called "Pay Yourself First", where you prioritize savings before accounting for any expenses.

2.4. Investments: The Growth Machine

Investments are aimed at creating wealth over the long term. They involve channeling your savings into channels like stocks, bonds, mutual funds or real estate which could produce returns and grow your wealth.

To maximize the potential of your investment, you need to understand the power of compounding – where the returns you earn on your investments further generate returns.

2.5. Budgeting: A Financial Compass

A budget is a plan that balances your income and expenses. It helps you prioritize spending, thereby making sure your financial goals are never sidetracked. Though there are several budgeting strategies, one of the most popular is the 50/30/20 rule:

1. 50% of income: Necessities

2. 30% of income: Discretionary expenses

3. 20% of income: Financial goals

2.6. Emergency Funds: The Financial Fire Extinguisher

An emergency fund is a separate savings account meant to cover unexpected expenses like medical emergencies or job loss. It gives you peace of mind and financial stability, enabling you to weather unforeseen circumstances without going into debt. A good rule of thumb is to have at least three to six months' worth of expenses in your emergency fund.

2.7. Insurance: Your Financial Shield

Insurance is a key component of financial planning. It safeguards your finances from unexpected life events, reducing the financial burdens. The most common types of insurances include health insurance, life insurance, home insurance, and auto insurance.

2.8. Tax Planning: A Necessary Chore

Understanding tax implications of your income and investments is vital to effectively manage your finances. Tax efficient investments like retirement accounts and certain mutual funds can help reduce your overall tax liability.

2.9. Retirement Planning: A Look into the Future

Retirement planning involves setting aside money today for your future when you no longer have a regular income. The earlier you begin the better, thanks to the power of compounding. Retirement plans like the 401(k) or Individual Retirement Account (IRA) are popular options due to their tax advantages.

Understanding these fundamental concepts of personal finance is the first step to ensuring a secure financial future. Once you have these basics down pat, you can then move on to more complex decisions such as choosing the right investments, strategizing your portfolio, and planning for long-term financial goals. The path to financial freedom starts here!

Chapter 3. Earning and Saving: The First Step

Money is a curious entity. We perceive it as a tangible material, yet its real value lies in its intangibility — in its capacity to blossom into a secure future, a better lifestyle, an ability to help others, and significantly, to provide a cushion for unforeseen circumstances. This transformative journey from tangible money to intangible value begins by mastering two simple yet powerful concepts — earning and saving.

3.1. The Miracle of Earnings

Earnings are the foundation of an investor's journey. They represent the rewards of your labor, skills and expertise. The concept of earnings goes beyond just your monthly paycheck. It encapsulates the capacious world of incomes through active work, passive incomes, and sometimes, even through windfalls. Your active income is the money earned by directly exchanging your time and effort, usually through a job or business. This forms the basic structure of your personal finance pyramid.

Passive income, on the other hand, is the money earned with little to no daily effort on your part. This could include returns from investments, rent from owned property, royalties, and more. Finally, there might be occasional windfalls - an inheritance, lottery, or any unexpected income. These earnings provide an added advantage and should be effectively managed.

To comprehend earnings better, let's break them down:

- Active Income:
- Job: Your salary, bonuses, allowances all fall under this category.

- Self-employment or business: If you run a business or are self-employed, your earnings from providing a service or selling a product come under active income.

- Passive Income:

- Investments: Returns or dividends from stocks, mutual funds and deposits fall in this category.

- Rent: Earnings from letting out a property or part of it.

- Royalties: If you hold a patent for an invention or have authored a book, the periodic payments you receive form part of the passive income.

- Windfall Income:

- Inheritance: It's the property or money you receive from someone, usually after their death.

- Lottery or winning a game show: While not common, these earnings do add substantially to your wealth.

Recognizing your sources of income and diversifying them enhances your earnings and reduces reliance on a single source. It doesn't matter how much you make; what counts is how you manage it to ensure its growth.

3.2. Harnessing the Power of Saving

Earning money is a fundamental step, but the magic truly begins with saving. Saving is the act of setting aside part of your income reserved for future use. The idea of saving might seem mundane; after all, it's just about not spending, right? But the truth is, saving is an art. It's the fine balance between fulfilling your immediate desires and securing a financially stable future.

Just like earnings, saving has its various components:

- Emergency fund: An emergency fund is a stash of money set

aside to cover the financial surprises life throws your way. These unexpected events can be stressful and costly. Having an emergency fund provides a financial safety net so you won't have to rely on credit cards or loans in times of crisis.

- Savings for goals: Saving is not just for emergencies; it's also for reaching larger life goals like buying a house, starting a business, or planning for your retirement.

- Investments: When you 'save' money by investing it, you're taking a further step to grow your wealth. Although investments are often associated with risks, they also offer substantial growth potential.

The key is to save before you spend. The sooner you start, the more money you'll have for emergency expenses, larger goals, and investments. Here's how you can make saving a habit:

- Pay yourself first: As soon as you get your salary or any form of income, immediately set aside a part of it for savings.

- Automate your savings: Automating your savings can make it easier to save money since you won't have to think about it every time you get paid.

- Track your expenses: It's essential to track where your money goes every month. This can provide insight into where you can cut back and save more.

- Set financial goals: Setting financial goals can give you something to strive for and motivate you to save more.

Mastering the art of saving positions you on a favorable path to wealth creation. Remember, it's not about how much money you earn, but how much you can save and grow.

3.3. From Earnings to Wealth

The journey from earning to saving to wealth creation is not a sprint but a marathon. Growing your wealth requires time, patience, and a fair understanding of your earnings and savings. Hence, as crucial as it is to improve your earnings and savings, it is just as important to manage them.

Remember, the goal is not just to secure a future, but to build one that aligns with your dreams and aspirations. Learning to navigate the world of earnings and savings is like learning to walk before you run. But once done, you can take decisive strides towards creating lasting wealth and financial independence. This journey could begin with the first step, the first penny saved, and a conscious commitment to secure a financially independent future.

Chapter 4. The Art of Budgeting: Making the Most of Your Money

Wonderfully, the cornerstone of any personal finance plan is a well-defined budget. A budget is the foundation upon which your road to financial independence and success will be built.

4.1. Understanding What A Budget Is

A budget, put simply, is a financial plan that helps you track your income and expenses. It's a blueprint for your financial life, akin to a roadmap for your journey. It guides you in understanding where your money comes from, where it goes, and most importantly, allows you to plan for its efficient utilization.

4.2. Why Do We Need a Budget?

The significance of a budget cannot be overstressed. Some of the essential functions it plays are:

1. Helping you spot areas where you are overspending
2. Guiding you in reflecting on your priorities and readjusting them if necessary
3. Providing a framework to save for future goals
4. Enabling you to find financial peace

Cultivating a habit of budgeting effectively keeps you in control of your finances, and ultimately, your life.

4.3. Fundamental Components of a Budget

The crux of any budget boils down to two primary elements: Income and Expenses.

Income includes the total money you receive from various sources like salary, investments, side-business, etc., while Expenses are divided into two main types:

1. Fixed Expenses: Rent or mortgage, car payments, insurance, etc.

2. Variable Expenses: Groceries, entertainment, discretionary spending, etc.

4.4. Creating Your First Budget

Getting started may seem daunting, but with methodical steps, it won't be. Here's a five-step plan to get you started:

1. Identify Your Income: Note down all your sources and the total amount of monthly income.

2. List Your Expenses: Categorize them as fixed or variable and list down everything.

3. Subtract Expenses from Income: This difference is what you have left to save or cover unexpected costs.

4. Set Financial Goals: They could be saving for a vacation, retirement or paying off loans.

5. Adjust Your Spending: If you are overspending, tweak your habits and routine to get back on track.

4.5. Upgrading Your Budget

As you grow financially and your income increases, your budget needs to evolve too. Start treating savings as a fixed expense. Add investing to your budget and let your money work for you.

Remember, budgeting is an iterative process. Update your budget as your income, expenses, and goals evolve.

4.6. Sticking to Your Budget

The success of a budget doesn't depend only on fancy spreadsheets or apps. It primarily hinges on your resolve to stick to it. Here are some strategies:

1. Budget for small pleasures: Completely depriving yourself often backfires. Instead, plan ahead for small indulgences.
2. Use technology: Apps can automate tracking and ease monitoring.
3. Keep goals in sight: Regularly remind yourself of the bigger picture to stay motivated.

4.7. The Role of Emergency Funds

Maintaining an emergency fund, ideally three to six months of living expenses, is vital. This fund acts as a financial safety net and should be part of your budget.

4.8. Beyond Budgeting

Achieving financial success certainly requires more than just a well-settled budget. Make sure after setting up a budget, you dive into the next chapters, like investing and wealth creation. But remember, it all starts with an effective budget.

This chapter painted a broad picture of budgeting's 'how' and 'why.' While it seems a skill requiring discipline and effort, the returns are undeniably fruitful. Making the most of your money is, after all, an art—one that begins with the simple act of budgeting.

Chapter 5. Introduction to Investing: Unraveling the Mystery

Welcome to the world of investing, where navigating the terrain might seem as hard as rocket science, but once you break it down to its basic elements, it suddenly morphs into something quite uncomplicated and, dare we say, exciting!

5.1. Understanding Investing

Imagine, for a moment, that you are a farmer. What would you do if you had a bag of seeds? You might eat some of them now, providing you with the nutrients you need right away. The rest, you could plant in a fertile field. These seeds will take time to grow, but when they do, you don't just get more seeds — you get an entire crop of them. Investing works in much the same way.

Simply put, investing is the act of committing money or capital to an endeavor with the expectation of obtaining an additional income or profit. Instead of consuming all your money now, you're planting it in the financial soil to grow your wealth over time. The whole premise of investing aligns with the philosophical mantra, "Don't eat your seed, rather sow it, reap lots more, and be merry in the future."

5.2. Why Invest?

Everyone acknowledges the importance of money in our lives. It offers us a certain degree of financial security and the ability to fulfil our needs and wants. However, merely saving money under the mattress is not enough. But why?

Well, it's due to a naughty little thing called inflation. Over time, the general price of goods and services tends to rise. As a result, the purchasing power of money erodes, meaning your money today will have lesser value in the future.

Investing your money not only ensures your financial growth but also helps protect the money you currently have from the harmful effects of inflation. With the right investments, your money lays golden eggs for you in the form of interest or dividends, growing your wealth and enabling you to realise your long-term financial goals.

5.3. Different Types of Investments

Investments are not just made in one way. In fact, when it comes to investing, you have a buffet of options available to you:

1. Stocks: These are shares in the ownership of a company and represent a claim on part of the company's assets and earnings.

2. Bonds: These are effectively loans, given by the buyer to the issuer in exchange for interest payments plus the return of the loan's face amount.

3. Mutual Funds: A mutual fund is a collection of stocks, bonds, or other securities owned by a group of investors and managed by a professional investment company.

These are just a few examples of the array of investment options at your plate—each comes with its own risks and rewards. Your choice should depend on your personal financial goals, risk appetite, and time horizon.

5.4. The Power of Compound Interest

Let's delve into one of the most fascinating aspects of investing: compound interest - the secret sauce that makes your money work for you. Simply put, compound interest is interest on interest.

To better visualize this, think of a small snowball rolling down a hill. As it rolls, it keeps gathering more snow and gets larger. In this analogy, the snowball is your initial investment, and the snow it gathers as it rolls downhill is the compound interest. Over time, a small snowball (or investment) can turn into a gigantic snowball (or a hefty sum of money).

Imagine you invest $10,000, and it grows by 5% each year. After the first year, you'll have $10,500. But the next year, you'll earn 5% on $10,500, so you'll have $11,025. This might not seem like a lot more, but when you extend that over 20 or 30 years, that base amount of $10,000 could grow exponentially thanks to compound interest.

Compound interest favors the patient. Remember, we're in it for the long haul!

5.5. Breaking the Investment Myths

However, certain myths around investing often scare away potential investors. Let's debunk a few right now!

- Myth: "Investing is just like gambling!" Reality: Unlike gambling, investing in the financial market involves making informed decisions based on market analysis and company performance. While there's risk involved, proper knowledge and strategic planning can lead to consistent returns over time.

- Myth: "Investing is only for the rich!" Reality: The investing world welcomes everyone with open arms, regardless of the size of their wallet. Platforms like mutual funds and Exchange-Traded Funds (ETFs) let you start investing with very little money.

- Myth: "Investing is too complex!" Reality: Any field appears daunting and complex when you're just dipping your toes in. With continuous learning, patience, and practice, you can become comfortable and adept over time.

Understanding the world of investing can seem like catching fish in the dark at first. But as you gather knowledge and gain confidence, you will begin to see the vast potential that investing holds. Remember, the fascinating world of investing is less about 'getting rich quick' and more about 'getting wealthy slowly.'

Welcome to this exciting journey. We don't promise it will always be smooth, but we can guarantee it will be enlightening and rewarding. After all, every journey starts with a single step. This is yours.

Chapter 6. Investment Instruments: Exploring Your Options

Investment Instruments are your primary tools in building your financial future. They are the vehicles which help you multiply your wealth. You have probably heard terms like stocks, bonds, mutual funds, and real estate, but do you know what they actually mean, their functioning, and the different risks associated with them? This chapter aims to demystify these asset types, covering their broad scope and characteristics.

6.1. Bonds - The Conservative Investor's Friend

Bonds are essentially loans that you, as an investor, give to the issuer. These issuers can be corporate entities or governmental bodies. When you buy a bond, you lend your money to the issuer for a certain period, known as the tenure. In return, the issuer promises to repay your initial investment (principle) upon maturity, plus regular interest (coupons).

Bonds are considered safer investment options with predictable returns, making them ideal for conservative risk-averse investors. These fixed-income instruments are best to create wealth incrementally yet steadily. However, bonds subject to interest rate risk, where if the rate increases, bond prices decrease.

6.2. Stocks - Riding the High Wave

Stocks represent ownership in a company's equity. Buying shares mean you own a proportionate part of the company. Stocks are high risk, yet they offer high potential returns. You can profit from stocks in two ways: dividends and capital gain. Dividends are part of the company's earnings distributed to shareholders. Capital gain arises when you sell your stocks at a higher price than it cost to buy them.

Despite their potential for high profits, stocks come with an increased risk. Stock prices can be volatile, and business or economic conditions affect them. The key here is to diversify the portfolio to minimize this risk and potentially increase returns.

6.3. Mutual Funds - Power of Pooling

In a mutual funds scheme, many investors pool in their money, and a professional fund manager then invests this pool into different asset classes. It's a hassle-free way to invest in the stock and bond market, bringing the benefits of diversification, expert management, and high liquidity.

Mutual funds provide a remarkable way to start investing, especially for those who lack the knowledge or time to manage their portfolio. They offer different types of schemes to cater to individuals with different risk appetites. However, since mutual funds are dependent on the market, they are exposed to the associated risks.

6.4. Real Estate - Tangible Asset Investment

Investing in real estate means acquiring physical land or property. It can offer regular income (rent) and capital appreciation over time. Real estate investment diversifies your portfolio, acts as a hedge against inflation, and provides tax benefits.

However, real estate requires huge initial capital, is illiquid, and managing property can be time-consuming. Moreover, the returns are uncertain as they depend on various factors like location, demand-supply dynamics, and economic conditions.

6.5. Derivatives - Hedging and Speculation Instruments

Derivatives are financial instruments whose value depends on an underlying asset – a share, bond, commodity, or currency. Options, futures, and swaps are a few examples of derivatives. They can be used for speculation (to profit from price movements) and to hedge risks.

Despite the potential for high profits, derivatives are complex and involve substantial risks. They're suitable for experienced investors who understand these risks, underlying assets, and the markets.

6.6. Commodities - The Gold, Oil and More

Commodities like gold, oil, agricultural products, etc., are basic goods used in commerce that are interchangeable with other goods of the same type. Commodity markets are usually volatile, influenced by supply and demand dynamics. They offer a good source of diversification as their prices are not directly correlated with stocks or bonds.

Investing in commodities, though it can provide inflation protection and portfolio diversification, can be risky due to high volatility. Direct ownership can be cumbersome, and futures contracts may be complex for a beginner.

6.7. Cryptocurrencies - The Digital Gold

Cryptocurrencies are virtual or digital currencies secured by cryptography. Bitcoin, Ethereum, and Ripple are a few well-known examples. Cryptocurrencies are highly volatile, making them risky yet potentially rewarding investments. They offer easy transfer of assets, the potential for high returns, and are attractive as a speculative asset.

Cryptocurrencies, however, are not regulated by any central authority. Their prices can be influenced by speculative trading, they can be susceptible to cyber threats, and they may also face regulatory issues.

Understanding these asset types and how they map to your risk profile, financial goals, and the market environment is crucial. Investing isn't about picking a random selection of these tools, but rather about which tool suits your unique needs the best. Remember, diversification is key in the long run, and understanding the instruments in your investment kit will help you ride the peaks and troughs of the market.

Chapter 7. Risk vs Reward: Balancing Your Investment Portfolio

Investing is both an exciting and daunting endeavour. This chapter will dive deep into two of the most critical aspects of investing: Risk and Reward. We'll explore various investment avenues, balance the scales between risks and rewards, and help you craft a personalized risk strategy that enhances your investment portfolio.

7.1. Understanding Risk and Reward

Risk and reward go hand-in-hand in the investment world. In simple terms, 'risk' refers to the possibility of your investment's actual return differing from the expected return, including the risk of losing the entire initial amount. 'Reward', on the other hand, corresponds to the potential profit or return you expect to receive on your investment.

Risk is an inherent part of investing. However, a higher risk is often associated with the possibility of higher returns, but with high enough risk the likelihood of loss also escalates. Thus, it's crucial to understand these concepts and strike a balance that accommodates your investment objectives, risk tolerance, and time horizons.

7.2. Building Blocks of Risk and Reward

To fundamentally understand risk and reward, let's break them down into smaller components.

1. **Risk Tolerance:** This is the level of risk you're comfortable with.

It's determined by a mix of your financial situation, age, investment goals, and your mental willingness to bear loss. Risk tolerance differs from person to person, and direct mapping of your risk tolerance will help categorize you as a conservative, moderate, or aggressive investor.

2. **Risk Capacity:** Unlike risk tolerance, risk capacity is the amount of risk you can afford to take, typically higher for individuals with more considerable assets and longer time horizons. This helps in determining how much risk is necessary for you to achieve your financial goals.

3. **Expected Reward:** This is the potential gain you anticipate on your investment.

4. **Actual Reward:** This is the real return you obtain from your investment. It can regress or surpass the expected reward.

7.3. Analyzing Risks

Investments come with different types such as market risk, credit risk, liquidity risk, and inflation risk, to name a few. Recognizing and analyzing these risks, and how they affect different asset classes, will help you curate a well-diversified portfolio.

1. **Market Risk:** This refers to the risk of investments declining due to economic developments or other events that impact the entire market.

2. **Credit Risk:** This involves potential losses due to an entity failing to live up to its contractual obligations.

3. **Liquidity Risk:** This is the risk of not being able to sell your investment at a fair price and get your money out when you want to.

4. **Inflation Risk:** This is the risk of loss in your purchasing power because the value of your investments does not keep up with inflation.

7.4. Methods to Mitigate Risks

Now that you've identified the various types of risk, here are a few strategic methods you can implement to mitigate them:

1. **Diversification:** By spreading your investments among various financial instruments, sectors, and geographies, you can reduce the impact of poor performance from a single investment.

2. **Regular Reviewing:** Investment reviews help you detect changes in market trends, alterations in risk factors, and shifts in your own financial goals.

3. **Asset Allocation:** Depending on your risk capacity and tolerance, devise an asset allocation strategy that suits your financial goals.

4. **Investing in Low-Risk Assets:** Investments like bonds, treasury bills, and fixed deposits provide lower returns but come with reduced risk levels.

7.5. Seeking Rewards

The allure of investing is the enticing rewards one can reap. However, it's essential to recognize that higher returns are generally associated with higher risk. Carefully consider your own risk tolerance before choosing investments with potentially higher returns. Maintain a diversified portfolio of low, medium, and high-risk assets based on your risk profile.

Achieving the perfect risk-reward balance may require adjustments and regular reviews of your investment portfolio. Always keep in mind that investing should be a long-term endeavor. Be patient, stay informed, and regularly reassess your investment plan as you traverse the path to your financial goals.

Chapter 8. The Power of Compound Interest: Money Making More Money

Understanding the concept of compound interest is a crucial first step in your investment journey. Often referred to as the eighth wonder of the world, it is the tool that will empower your money to make more money over time.

8.1. The Basics: How Compound Interest Works

Compound interest is the interest on a loan or deposit that is calculated based on the initial principal, and the accumulated interest from previous periods. To put it simply, compound interest lets you earn interest on your interest. Unlike simple interest, which only grows linearly, compound interest grows exponentially, accelerating the growth of your wealth.

To illustrate, let's imagine you deposit $1,000 into a savings account that compounds annually at a 5% interest rate. At the end of the first year, you'll have $1,050 - your original $1,000 plus $50 in interest. The following year, you are not just earning interest on your original $1,000, but also the $50 interest from the first year. Therefore, you'll earn $52.50 in interest, bringing your total to $1,102.50. As this cycle repeats over time, your money grows at an ever-accelerating rate.

The formula for compound interest is as follows:

$$A = P (1 + r/n) \wedge (nt)$$

where: - A is the amount of money accumulated after n years, including interest. - P is the principal amount (the initial amount of money). - r is the annual interest rate (in decimal). - n is the number of times that interest is compounded per year. - t is the time the money is invested or borrowed for, in years.

8.2. The Time Value of Money

To fully exploit the power of compound interest, one needs to understand the time value of money (TVM). The TVM concept implies that money available at the present time is worth more than the same amount in the future due to its potential earning capacity. This core principle states that, provided money can earn interest, any amount of money is worth more the sooner it is received.

Together, TVM and compound interest emphasize the importance of starting to invest as soon as possible. The longer your money is invested, the greater the compounding effects, and the larger your investment will grow.

8.3. Effects of Compounding Frequency

The compounding frequency, i.e., the number of times interest is calculated and added back to the principal in a given time period, also plays a huge role in the final value of an investment. The same principal amount and interest rate can yield different amounts based on whether the interest is compounded annually, semi-annually, quarterly, monthly, or even daily.

The more frequently interest is compounded, the greater the overall return will be. However, the converse is also true. More frequent compounding means paying more interest on loans. As an investor, you should always be aware of the compounding frequency when comparing different investment options.

8.4. The Power of Compounding on Various Types of Investments

Compound interest doesn't just apply to savings accounts. It plays a significant role in various types of investments, such as stocks, bonds, mutual funds, and real estate.

When investing in stocks that pay dividends, if you choose to reinvest those dividends, they will also earn returns. Over time, and with the power of compounding, this can significantly increase your total return.

Similarly, with bonds, if you reinvest the interest you receive instead of spending it, you can buy more bonds, which will yield more interest.

In a mutual fund, the profit from the fund's investments can be reinvested, further increasing the amount of shares you own. The increased number of shares will generate more profit, and this cycle can continue, exponentially increasing your return on investment over time.

8.5. Power of Starting Early

The power of compound interest is more impactful the earlier you start investing. An early start gives you a considerable advantage as you will be giving your money more time to grow.

To illustrate, suppose Person A starts investing $200 per month at age 25, expecting an annual return of 7%. If they continue doing this until they are 65, their investment will grow to approximately $525,000. On the other hand, if Person B starts doing the same research and making the same investments at age 35, their investment amount at age 65 would be less than $245,000. That's a huge difference of $280,000 just because Person A started 10 years earlier.

8.6. Patience and Discipline

Harnessing the power of compound interest requires patience and discipline. Patience to allow the compound effect to happen and discipline to keep investing consistently over time.

Investing is a long-term game. The longer you leave your investment to grow, the more potent the compound effect will be. Remember, we're talking years or even decades here, not mere weeks or months.

8.7. Wrapping It Up

Understanding the power of compound interest is a substantial piece of the investing puzzle. It's what makes investing, particularly early on, such a potent avenue to grow wealth over the long term. Starting early, staying consistent with your investments, and waiting patiently will allow you to maximize the power of compound interest and set a strong foundation for a prosperous financial future.

Chapter 9. Retirement Planning: Fostering Financial Security for Future

Retirement may seem like a stage of life that's eons away, but it is an indisputable truth that advanced planning is the key to ensuring a comfortable and secure post-retirement life. Far from being a subject of concern and anxiety, visioning and preparing for your retirement can be an exciting journey, promising a fulfilling and rich life beyond your working years.

9.1. Understanding Retirement Planning

Retirement Planning is about setting your financial goals for the retirement life you envision and then deciding on the necessary steps to achieve these goals. It includes determining retirement expenses based on your desired lifestyle, identifying income sources, setting aside savings, and managing assets and risk. It's about creating a financial cushion that helps you maintain your lifestyle without regular employment income.

The process of retirement planning starts with establishing long-term financial goals. These goals are unique to each individual or family, based on factors such as current lifestyle, expected retirement age, health, expected life span, and personal aspirations. No two people's retirement plans will look exactly the same because everyone's circumstances differ.

9.2. Factors Influencing Retirement Planning

Several factors come into play while planning one's retirement. Some of them include:

1. Retirement Age: The age at which you plan to retire directly impacts your retirement planning; the earlier you want to retire, the larger the corpus required.

2. Life Expectancy: Longevity risk, the risk of outliving your savings, is a real concern for many retirees. Consider this when deciding how much to save for retirement.

3. Inflation: Inflation causes a decrease in purchasing power. Your retirement corpus should account for increasing costs over the years.

4. Health Care Costs: As we age, health issues usually crop up, and treating them can be expensive. Health insurance and emergency funds for medical expenses should be part of your retirement plan.

5. Lifestyle: Your planned retirement lifestyle—traveling, indulging in hobbies, etc.—will determine how much money you need to set aside.

6. Social Security: The amount you expect to receive from Social Security or other Government schemes will factor into your retirement planning.

9.3. The Importance of Starting Early

The earlier you start your retirement planning, the larger the investment corpus that can be built with less financial strain. This is because of the magic of compounding, where you earn interest on the interest your investment has already earned. Starting early allows your savings to grow exponentially over time, providing a larger nest egg for your sunset years.

For instance, if you start investing $200 per month at the age of 25, with an annual return of 8%, by the time you reach 65, you'll have about $700,000 saved up, whereas if you start investing the same amount at the age of 35, you'll have accumulated around $300,000 only. That's less than half, and it demonstrates vividly the power of starting early.

9.4. Creating a Retirement Plan

1. Determine Your Retirement Income Needs: Decide what kind of lifestyle you wish to live and estimate the amount it will cost.

2. Evaluate Your Current Assets and Income: Assess what you currently have, including savings, assets, and sources of income.

3. Develop a Savings Plan: Based on your needs and resources, create a savings plan. Consider options like employer-sponsored retirement plans, IRAs or personal savings.

4. Allocate Your Investments: Diversify your portfolio according to your risk tolerance and time horizon.

5. Plan for Emergencies: Unexpected situations can arise. A reserve fund is crucial to ensure such situations do not disrupt your retirement plan.

6. Review & Adjust Regularly: Periodically evaluate your retirement plan to adjust for changing circumstances or goals.

9.5. Risk Management in Retirement Planning

It's important to have the right balance between risk and reward in your retirement planning. An overly aggressive strategy may have high potential returns but could equally lead to significant losses, whereas a very conservative strategy may not yield the returns required to meet your retirement goals. Based on your risk tolerance, diversify your portfolio across asset classes like bonds, stocks, and mutual funds.

Insurance also plays a significant role in risk management and retirement planning. Life insurance helps your family maintain their lifestyle even in the unfortunate event of your demise, while health insurance covers high medical costs, a concern as people age.

9.6. Beyond Monetary Aspects

There's more to retirement planning than just financial issues. It also includes planning your time, deciding where to live, maintaining health, and building a social support system. Take some time to reflect on these matters too and make this particular chapter of life as fulfilling as possible.

Retirement planning is a long-term commitment that pays off in peace of mind, security, and financial independence in your golden years. It's never too late to start, but starting early provides a significant advantage. Make your move today.

Chapter 10. Tax Planning and Insurance: Navigating the Essentials

Understanding the tax system and the role insurance plays in your financial planning is a critical step on your investment journey. These financial tools not only aid in ensuring a secure financial future, they can also provide attractive tax benefits.

10.1. The Tax System and You

First, let's understand the tax system. Taxes are an unavoidable aspect of earning money, and since everyone must pay them, it's vital to have an understanding of how they impact your personal finances.

In many countries, taxes are progressive, meaning the rate increases as the taxable amount increases. These rates depend on your annual income, and the tax slabs are periodically revised by the government.

Let's look at an example structure (note: actual rates may vary based on your country):

- Income up to $20,000: 0%

- Income from $20,001 to $50,000: 10%

- Income from $50,001 to $100,000: 20%

- Income over $100,000: 30%

These rates are important as they help you understand how much of your income goes towards paying taxes.

The good news is there are ways to reduce your taxable income legally, and that's where tax planning comes in.

10.2. Understanding Tax Planning

Tax planning is a legal way of reducing your tax liability through the use of various concessions and deductions provided by the government. The goal is to arrange your financial affairs in a way that minimizes your taxes.

There are multiple methods to save on tax under various sections of the tax law. Here are some popular ways:

1. Investment in tax-saving instruments: The government provides tax breaks on certain investments like retirement savings, health insurance premiums, etc.

2. Home loans: The principal and interest repayment on your home loan comes with tax benefits.

3. Education loans: The interest repaid on an education loan is eligible for a tax deduction.

4. Charitable Contributions: Donations to approved charitable organizations can also result in substantial tax breaks.

Understanding which tax breaks apply to your specific situation can lead to substantial savings.

10.3. The Role of Insurance in Tax Planning

Another important instrument in your tax planning strategy is insurance. Insurance is not just about protecting you and your loved ones; it acts as an effective tool to reduce your tax liability.

Insurance premiums for policies such as life insurance and health insurance usually qualify for tax deductions. This means the money spent on these premiums can be subtracted from your gross income when calculating your taxable income. Various insurance policies come with different tax benefits.

Let's delve deeper into some commonly used insurance types for tax saving.

10.4. Life Insurance

Life insurance provides financial protection to your family in case of your untimely demise. It's an essential part of every well-rounded financial plan. Beyond its immediate purpose, life insurance policies can also be used for efficient tax planning.

The premiums paid towards life insurance are eligible for tax deductions. This applies for policies in the name of the taxpayer, spouse, or children.

10.5. Health Insurance

Health insurance plays a critical role in managing health-related costs. With the ever-rising healthcare costs, buying a health insurance policy has never been more critical. Like life insurance, health insurance premiums qualify for tax deductions.

Tax benefits vary and depend on the policyholder's age and whether the insurance is for self, spouse, children, or dependent parents.

10.6. Understanding the Insurance-Cum-Investment Options

Certain insurance policies are packaged as investment products, such as Unit Linked Insurance Plans (ULIPs) and Endowment Policies. These plans serve dual purposes - providing a life cover and acting as an investment tool.

The premiums paid towards these policies are eligible for tax deductions. The added advantage is that the returns generated from such insurance policies are also tax-free.

Although these insurance-cum-investment options could potentially offer higher returns, carefully consider their higher charges, lock-in period, and risks compared to pure investment or pure insurance products.

10.7. Final Thoughts

Tax planning should not be an afterthought; instead, it should be integrated into your financial strategy from the start. By utilizing tax-saving instruments and insurance policies wisely, you can significantly reduce your tax liability and increase your net income.

Remember, the wise investor is not the one who makes the most significant income but the one who effectively keeps the most income.

Insurance, on the other hand, provides a much-needed safety net while also contributing to tax savings. Therefore, understanding how these two aspects can work in your favor will help secure your financial future.

Finally, tax laws and insurance policies can be complex and ever-changing. Keeping yourself updated and seeking professional advice when in doubt can go a long way in preserving and growing your wealth.

This chapter has equipped you with a fundamental understanding of tax planning and insurance basics. As you navigate your financial journey, use this knowledge as your guide to securing a well-planned, insured, and tax-efficient future.

Chapter 11. Advanced Investment Strategies: Mastering Your Financial Future

Let's set the stage; you have a firm grasp of the basics - understanding risk, types, and the time value of money. Now it's time to pull back the curtain on more complex investment strategies. As we prepare, remember these two key principles: investing is about both managing risk and maximizing returns, and knowledge is your most valuable asset.

11.1. Understanding Leverage

Leverage is one of the most misunderstood concepts in investing, despite being a powerful tool. It refers to using borrowed capital for investment under the expectation the investment's returns will be more than the cost of borrowing. It's like weightlifting for your financial portfolio - the results can be substantial, but you must handle the weights (debt) carefully to prevent unnecessary pain.

The effectiveness of leverage depends on the return rate of the investment and the borrowing rate. If we can achieve a return higher than the cost of borrowing, leverage works in our favor, but the reverse can exacerbate losses. In essence, leverage magnifies both potential profits and losses.

11.2. Portfolio Diversification

Don't put all your eggs in one basket - we've all heard the saying. Portfolio diversification embodies this idea. It's a risk management strategy that involves mixing various investments within a portfolio.

Diversification intends to hold assets differing in risk levels and potential returns. This strategy helps to reduce the impact of poor-performing investments. They're buffered by other investments' performance, creating a risk-return trade-off. A diversified portfolio could include different assets such as stocks, bonds, and real estate, across different industries, geographic regions, and company sizes.

11.3. Understanding Options

Options are another higher-level investment strategy that requires a sophisticated understanding of the market. These financial instruments give you the right, but not obligation, to buy (call option) or sell (put option) an asset at a set price before a specified date.

Options can be leveraged for various investment stratagems. They allow investors to hedge against potential losses in other investments, speculate on the future direction of markets, or earn premiums. However, because of their complexities and inherent risk, options are typically recommended for more seasoned investors.

11.4. Exchange-Traded Funds (ETFs) and Index Funds

Enter the world of ETFs and Index funds: widely diversified, low-cost alternatives to individual stock picking. ETFs are marketable securities that track an index, sector, commodity, or a variety of other assets. Index funds follow specific indexes like the S&P 500.

ETFs and Index funds offer a passive investment strategy - you're simply replicating the performance of a particular index. While the possibility of dramatically outperforming the market is lower, these instruments mitigate risk through diversification and are ideal for those seeking to generate steady, long-term returns. They're a popular choice among advanced and novice investors alike due to their lower expense ratios and broader market exposure.

11.5. Income Investing

Income investing is a strategy focused on building a portfolio of income-generating assets. This strategy often appeals to those at or near retirement, but it can be beneficial at any life stage. The objective is to create a steady stream of income through dividends and interest payments instead of relying on capital gains.

This strategy often involves investing in stable, dividend-paying companies, bonds, and real estate investments. These investments usually prioritize consistent returns over the volatility of the broader market.

11.6. Rebalancing Your Portfolio

Diversification isn't a one-and-done deal. Over time, market movements can lead to your investments becoming unaligned with your original allocation strategy. To rectify this, you need to rebalance your portfolio. This involves selling off investments in over-weighted areas and purchasing in under-weighted ones.

It's recommended that you review and potentially rebalance your portfolio annually or anytime your financial objectives change. Remember, rebalancing can have tax implications, so consult a financial advisor beforehand.

11.7. Tax Efficient Investing

Investing isn't solely about generating returns but also managing how much of those returns you get to keep after-tax. Tax-efficient investing aims to minimize tax liability through strategic decisions like using tax-advantaged accounts, holding investments long enough to qualify for long-term capital gains rates, and considering the tax implications of selling investments.

Advanced investment strategies aren't about rushing in to make quick returns. They're about understanding the landscape, measuring risks, calculating potential benefits, and taking decisive action. With these strategies, you're equipped to grow and protect your wealth, fostering a financial future where you're in control. Whether you're bullish, bearish, or biding your time, remember: no investment journey is without risk, but with risk, comes reward. Now, go embark on your personal finance adventure with newfound know-how and confidence.

www.ingramcontent.com/pod-product-compliance
Lightning Source LLC
Chambersburg PA
CBHW062310290526
45794CB00006B/2741